J

Come! Sit! Speak!

By Charnan Simon

Illustrated by
Bari Weissman

Children's Press®
A Division of Scholastic Inc.
New York Toronto London Auckland Sydney
Mexico City New Delhi Hong Kong
Danbury, Connecticut

For the real Ariel and Hana, best
friends sometimes and forever

C. S.

To my mom, with love

B. W.

Reading Consultant:

Linda Cornwell
Learning Resource Consultant
Indiana Department of Education

Library of Congress Cataloging-in-Publication Data
Simon, Charnan.
Come! Sit! Speak! / by Charnan Simon ; illustrated by Bari Weissman.
p. cm. — (Rookie reader)
Summary: Ariel Kazunas wants a puppy but gets a baby sister instead.
ISBN 0-516-20397-5 (lib.bdg.)   0-516-26250-5 (pbk.)
[1. Babies—Fiction. 2. Sisters—Fiction. 3. Dogs—Fiction.]
I. Weissman, Bari, ill. II. Title. III. Series.
PZ7.S6035Co 1997
[E] —dc21
                              96-49440
                              CIP
                              AC

© 1997 by Charnan Simon
Illustration © 1997 by Bari Weissman

Ariel Kazunas
wanted a puppy.

Instead, she got a baby sister.

5

"No fair!" said Ariel.

6

"I could teach
a puppy tricks.

A puppy would
be my friend."

"Baby Hana will
be your friend,"
said her mother.

9

"You can teach your sister everything," said her father.

11

Ariel thought about this.

13

Then she got to work.

16

21

Her parents were surprised
at what a good teacher
Ariel was.

27

Now Ariel has a best friend AND a puppy.

28

30

She is still
a very good teacher.

Word List (64 words)

a	fetch	over	this
about	friend	parents	thought
and	good	pony	to
Ariel	got	puppy	tricks
at	Hana	roll	very
baby	has	said	want
be	her	she	wanted
beg	I	sister	was
best	instead	sit	we
can	is	speak	were
come	Kazunas	stay	what
could	know	still	will
do	mother	surprised	work
everything	my	teach	would
fair	no	teacher	you
father	now	then	your

About the Author

Charnan Simon lives in Madison, Wisconsin with her husband, Tom Kazunas, and her daughters, Ariel and Hana. Ariel really did teach Hana everything she needed to know when she was a baby. Today, Ariel and Hana really do have a dog, Sam, whom they love dearly. Ms. Simon enjoys spending time with her family and reading and writing books.

About the Illustrator

Bari Weissman grew up in New York City. She has been illustrating for more than twenty years. She and her husband, Warren, live in Boston, Massachusetts with Ida and Ishy (their dog and cat), who come, sit, and speak only when they want to!